stay hopeful and optimistic. God knows that your future is bright, and I pray that you'll know it too.

Let us hold fast the confession of our hope without wavering, for He who promised is faithful.

HEBREWS 10:23 NASB

Our prospects are as bright as the promises of God.

ADONIRAM JUDSON

I prayed for your future today. Then I remembered that your future is already secure. I hope you remember it, too.

And God is able to make all grace abound to you,
so that always having all sufficiency in everything,
you may have an abundance for every good deed.

2 CORINTHIANS 9:8 NASB

*Knowing that your future
is absolutely assured can free you
to live abundantly today.*

SARAH YOUNG

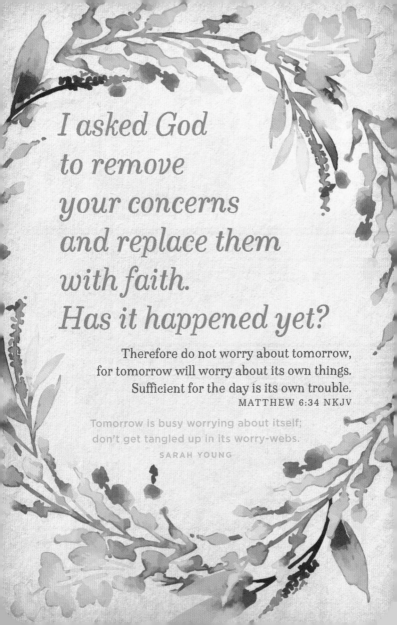

I asked God
to remove
your concerns
and replace them
with faith.
Has it happened yet?

Therefore do not worry about tomorrow,
for tomorrow will worry about its own things.
Sufficient for the day is its own trouble.
MATTHEW 6:34 NKJV

Tomorrow is busy worrying about itself;
don't get tangled up in its worry-webs.
SARAH YOUNG

Today, I asked God to fill
your mind with good thoughts.
I know my prayer
will be answered soon.
Immediately would be nice.

Finally brothers, whatever is true,
whatever is honorable, whatever is just, whatever is pure,
whatever is lovely, whatever is commendable—
if there is any moral excellence and if there is any praise—
dwell on these things.

PHILIPPIANS 4:8 HCSB

It is the thoughts and intents of the heart that shape a person's life.
JOHN ELDREDGE

Nothing is too hard for God,
and miracles happen every day.
Big miracles.
Little miracles.
In-between ones, too.
I'm praying for yours.

———

*No eye has seen, no ear has heard,
no mind has conceived what God has prepared
for those who love him.*
1 CORINTHIANS 2:9 NIV

———

It is wonderful what miracles God works
in wills that are utterly surrendered to Him.
HANNAH WHITALL SMITH

I pray that you'll experience God's peace today. And every day after day after that.

Peace I leave with you, My peace I give to you; not as the world gives do I give to you. Let not your heart be troubled, neither let it be afraid.

JOHN 14:27 NKJV

God's power is great enough for our deepest needs. You can go on. You can pick up the pieces and start anew. You can face your fears. You can find peace. You can have courage. There is healing for your soul.

SUZANNE DALE EZELL

Today, I asked the Lord
to remind you that
He is your shepherd.
You're safe with Him.
Very safe.

But as it is written: What no eye has seen
and no ear has heard, and what has never
come into a man's heart, is what God has
prepared for those who love Him.

1 CORINTHIANS 2:9 HCSB

Faith is not merely holding on to
God. It is God holding on to you.
CORRIE TEN BOOM

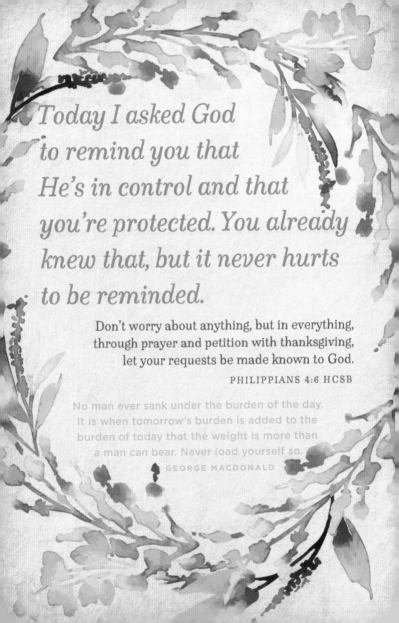

Today I asked God
to remind you that
He's in control and that
you're protected. You already
knew that, but it never hurts
to be reminded.

Don't worry about anything, but in everything,
through prayer and petition with thanksgiving,
let your requests be made known to God.

PHILIPPIANS 4:6 HCSB

No man ever sank under the burden of the day.
It is when tomorrow's burden is added to the
burden of today that the weight is more than
a man can bear. Never load yourself so.

GEORGE MACDONALD

Step by step, you're going to make it. I asked God to give you patience until you get there.

It is better to be patient than powerful; it is better to have self-control than to conquer a city.

PROVERBS 16:32 NLT

Faith does not concern itself with the entire journey. One step is enough.

LETTIE COWMAN

When you follow
in Christ's footsteps,
you're always on the right path.
I'm praying for your journey.

———

"Follow Me," He told them,
"and I will make you fishers of men!"
Immediately they left their nets and followed Him.

MATTHEW 4:19-20 HCSB

———

Jesus gives us hope because He keeps us company,
has a vision and knows the way we should go.

MAX LUCADO

I pray that you'll trust yourself and your Father in heaven. But not necessarily in that order.

You are my hope; O Lord GOD,
You are my confidence.

PSALM 71:5 NASB

Faith in God is the greatest power,
but great, too, is faith in oneself.

MARY MCLEOD BETHUNE

*I asked God
to remind you that
He is with you always.
He's not just near.
He's here.
Always.*

Do not be afraid or discouraged. For the
LORD your God is with you wherever you go.

JOSHUA 1:9 NLT

*Mark it down.
You will never go
where God is not.*
MAX LUCADO

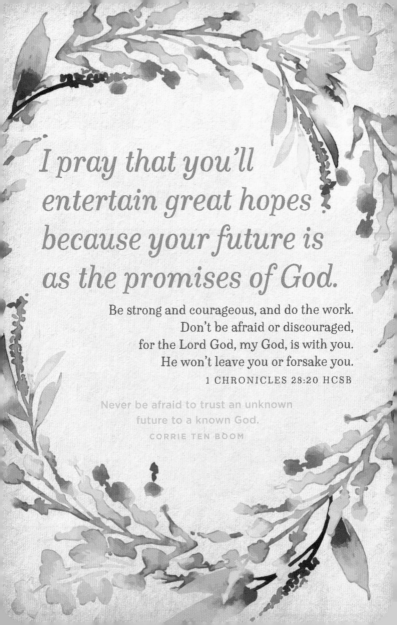

I pray that you'll entertain great hopes because your future is as the promises of God.

Be strong and courageous, and do the work.
Don't be afraid or discouraged,
for the Lord God, my God, is with you.
He won't leave you or forsake you.

1 CHRONICLES 28:20 HCSB

Never be afraid to trust an unknown
future to a known God.

CORRIE TEN BOOM

DaySpring

I asked God to remind you
that He's always available.
24/7. 365.
He's our eternal Shepherd,
and He knows the right path...
by heart.

The LORD says, "I will guide you along the best pathway
for your life. I will advise you and watch over you."
PSALM 32:8 NLT

Often God has to shut a door in our face so that he can
subsequently open the door through which he wants us to go.
CATHERINE MARSHALL

There's only one you in God's
phonebook, and He's calling.
I'm praying that you'll answer.
Today would be nice.

———

I remind you to fan into flame the gift of God.
2 TIMOTHY 1:6 NIV

———

You aren't an accident. You were deliberately
planned, specifically gifted, and lovingly positioned
on this earth by the Master Craftsman.
MAX LUCADO

DaySpring

I'm praying
that you'll stay positive.
And, I'm praying
you'll remember God
has big plans for you.
Because He does.

Anything is possible
if a person believes.
MARK 9:23 NLT

Optimism is that faith
that leads to achievement.
HELEN KELLER

DaySpring

*Today, I prayed
that you'd be filled
with hope and assurance.
God is by your side,
now and forever,
so you can live courageously.
Now and forever.*

And God, in his mighty power,
will protect you until you receive this
salvation, because you are trusting him.

1 PETER 1:5 NLT

*Never be afraid to trust an
unknown future to a known God.*
CORRIE TEN BOOM

DaySpring

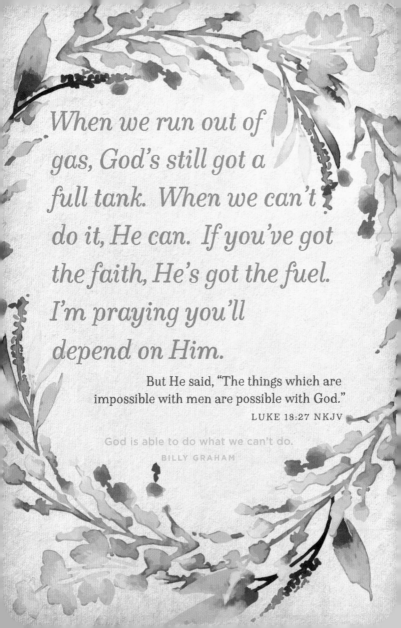

When we run out of gas, God's still got a full tank. When we can't do it, He can. If you've got the faith, He's got the fuel. I'm praying you'll depend on Him.

But He said, "The things which are impossible with men are possible with God."

LUKE 18:27 NKJV

God is able to do what we can't do.

BILLY GRAHAM

DaySpring

I asked God to remind you that He's bringing new opportunities to your door. When He knocks, as He most certainly will, I pray that you'll answer Him with a smile.

This is the day the Lord has made;
let us rejoice and be glad in it.
PSALM 118:24 HCSB

Life is a glorious opportunity.
BILLY GRAHAM

DaySpring

I prayed for you today,
and for your new endeavor.
I asked God to keep you
in the palm of His hand.
Just thought you'd want to know.

———

There is one thing I always do.
Forgetting the past and straining toward
what is ahead, I keep trying to reach the goal
and get the prize for which God called me . . .
PHILIPPIANS 3:13-14 NCV

———

Begin where we will, God is there first.
A. W. TOZER

Today, I talked to God
about your dreams.
I asked Him to help you
make them come true.
And I believe He will.
So keep dreaming. Big.

The Lord bless you and protect
you; the Lord make His face shine
on you, and be gracious to you.
NUMBERS 6:24-25 HCSB

Since it doesn't cost a dime to dream,
you'll never shortchange yourself when
you stretch your imagination.
ROBERT SCHULLER

I asked God to give you
hope for the future
and courage for your journey.
If you feel it, let me know.
If not, I'll keep praying.

Happy is the one whose help is the God of
Jacob, whose hope is in the Lord his God.

PSALM 146:5 HCSB

God rarely makes
our fear disappear.
Instead, he asks us
to be strong and
take courage.
BRUCE WILKINSON

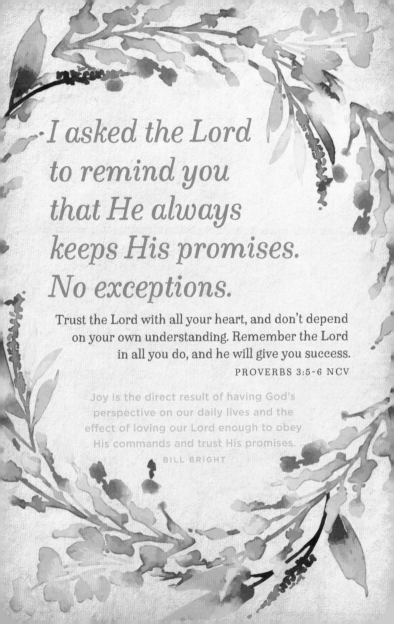

I asked the Lord to remind you that He always keeps His promises. No exceptions.

Trust the Lord with all your heart, and don't depend on your own understanding. Remember the Lord in all you do, and he will give you success.

PROVERBS 3:5-6 NCV

Joy is the direct result of having God's perspective on our daily lives and the effect of loving our Lord enough to obey His commands and trust His promises.

BILL BRIGHT

DaySpring

You've been dreaming
about this adventure,
and now you've begun.
Congratulations!
I'm praying for you.

Then the One seated on the throne said, "Look!
I am making everything new."
REVELATION 21:5 HCSB

If you can dream it, you can do it.
WALT DISNEY

I asked God to remind you that faith moves mountains. Then, when I finished praying, I had this funny feeling that your mountains are starting to move.

I tell you the truth, if you have faith as small as a mustard seed, you can say to this mountain, "Move from here to there" and it will move. Nothing will be impossible for you.

MATTHEW 17:20 NIV

Faith is a strong power, mastering any difficulty in the strength of the Lord who made heaven and earth.

CORRIE TEN BOOM

DaySpring

God can do anything and heal anybody. And I pray that you'll never forget it.

Is anything too hard for the Lord?

GENESIS 18:14 NKJV

God's specialty is raising dead things to life and making impossible things possible. You don't have the need that exceeds His power.

BETH MOORE

DaySpring

*I asked God
to comfort you today.
I'm sure He heard my prayer.
So, open your heart to Him.
ASAP.*

As for God, His way is perfect;

the word of the Lord is proven;

He is a shield to all who trust in Him.

PSALM 18:30 NKJV

*When once we are assured
that God is good, then there
can be nothing left to fear.*
HANNAH WHITALL SMITH

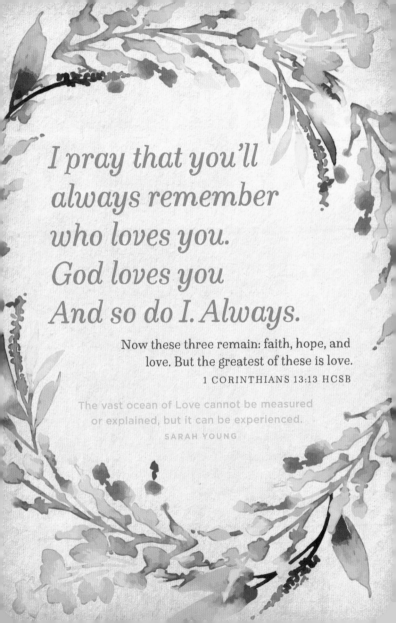

I pray that you'll always remember who loves you. God loves you And so do I. Always.

Now these three remain: faith, hope, and love. But the greatest of these is love.

1 CORINTHIANS 13:13 HCSB

The vast ocean of Love cannot be measured or explained, but it can be experienced.

SARAH YOUNG

*I pray that you'll
keep looking ahead.
Your future is bright
and God is ready to help.
Congratulations on your
next grand adventure.*

The Lord says, "Forget what happened before, and do not
think about the past. Look at the new thing I am going
to do. It is already happening. Don't you see it? I will
make a road in the desert and rivers in the dry land."

ISAIAH 43:18-19 NCV

*You must learn, you must let God teach you, that the only way to get
rid of your past is to make a future out of it. God will waste nothing.*

PHILLIPS BROOKS

DaySpring

If you ever feel like you've been backed into a corner, remember that you've got plenty of praying friends in your corner. Including me.

———

A friend loves at all times, and a brother is born for adversity.

PROVERBS 17:17 NIV

———

Never bend your head. Always hold it high. Look the world straight in the eye.

HELEN KELLER

DaySpring

Today, I prayed that you'll stay strong and courageous, knowing that you and God, working together, can get the job done.

The Lord is my light and my salvation—whom should I fear? The Lord is the stronghold of my life—of whom should I be afraid?

PSALM 27:1 HCSB

Discipline yourself to stay close to God. He alone is your security.

BILLY GRAHAM

DaySpring

You're getting closer to the finish line. I asked God to help you finish strong and soon.

Let us not become weary in doing good,
for at the proper time we
will reap a harvest if we do not give up.

GALATIANS 6:9 NIV

*We are all on our way
somewhere. We'll get there
if we just keep going.*
BARBARA JOHNSON

DaySpring

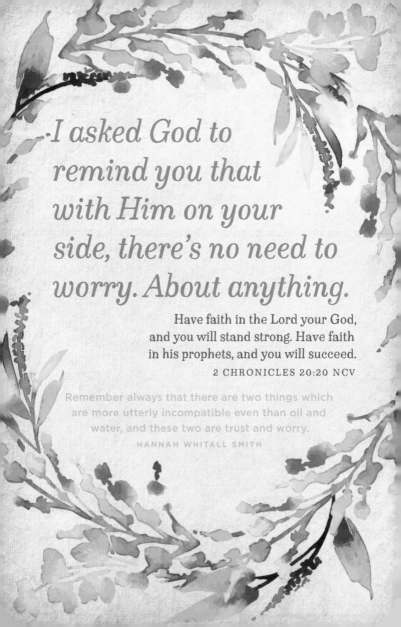

I asked God to remind you that with Him on your side, there's no need to worry. About anything.

Have faith in the Lord your God, and you will stand strong. Have faith in his prophets, and you will succeed.

2 CHRONICLES 20:20 NCV

Remember always that there are two things which are more utterly incompatible even than oil and water, and these two are trust and worry.

HANNAH WHITALL SMITH

DaySpring

I'm praying
for your journey.
God will be with you
every step of the way.
Always let Him lead.

The LORD says, "I will guide you along the best pathway
for your life. I will advise you and watch over you."

PSALM 32:8 NLT

When we are obedient, God guides our steps and our stops.

CORRIE TEN BOOM

DaySpring

I asked God to remind you
that no job is too big for Him.
I'm sure you already knew
that, but it never hurts
to be reminded.

This hope we have as an anchor of the
soul, a hope both sure and steadfast.
HEBREWS 6:19 NASB

The earth's troubles fade in the light of heaven's hope.
BILLY GRAHAM

DaySpring

Today, I prayed for you
to stay strong.
There's nothing you'll face today
that you and God,
working together, can't handle.

Search for the Lord and for his
strength, and keep on searching.
Think of the wonderful works he
has done, the miracles and the
judgments he handed down.

PSALM 105:4-5 NLT

God will give us the strength and resources we need
to live through any situation in life that He ordains.

BILLY GRAHAM

Today, I asked God to shower
you with His abundance
So don't worry if you see
a few storm clouds overhead.
They're probably just
showers of blessings.

I am come that they might have life, and
that they might have it more abundantly.

JOHN 10:10 KJV

God is the giver, and we are the receivers.
And His richest gifts are bestowed
not upon those who do the greatest things,
but upon those who accept
His abundance and His grace.
HANNAH WHITALL SMITH

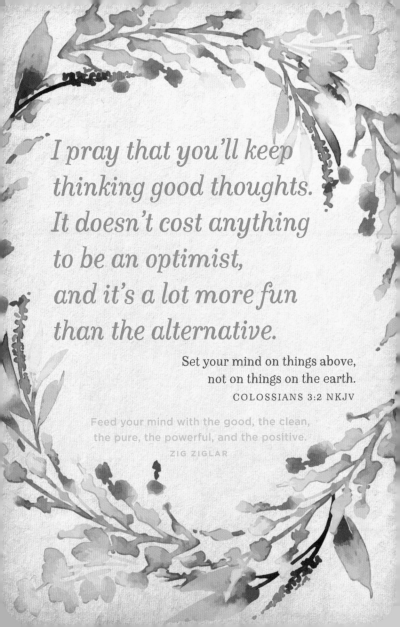

I pray that you'll keep
thinking good thoughts.
It doesn't cost anything
to be an optimist,
and it's a lot more fun
than the alternative.

Set your mind on things above,
not on things on the earth.
COLOSSIANS 3:2 NKJV

Feed your mind with the good, the clean,
the pure, the powerful, and the positive.
ZIG ZIGLAR

Life can be difficult,
choices can be hard,
and we all make mistakes.
God has forgiven you,
and I pray that you will, too.

Let us, then, feel very sure that we can come before
God's throne where there is grace. There we can receive
mercy and grace to help us when we need it.
HEBREWS 4:16 NCV

If God forgives us and we do not forgive ourselves, we
make ourselves greater than God.
EDWIN LOUIS COLE

We're thankful for you,
and we're praying for you.
A lot.

---

*I will thank the Lord with all my heart; I
will declare all Your wonderful works. I
will rejoice and boast about You; I will
sing about Your name, Most High.*

PSALM 9:1-2 HCSB

God knows everything. He can manage
everything, and He loves us. Surely this is enough
for a fullness of joy that is beyond words.

HANNAH WHITALL SMITH

DaySpring

I asked God to give you wisdom for the decisions ahead. I knew that you could make good choices, but I figured that you and God would make great ones.

But if any of you lacks wisdom, let him ask of God, who gives to all generously and without reproach, and it will be given to him.

JAMES 1:5 NASB

God, give us the grace to accept with serenity the things that cannot be changed, the courage to change the things that should be changed, and the wisdom to distinguish the one from the other.

REINHOLD NIEBUHR

*Every day,
including this one,
is a chance to begin
something new.
I'm praying
for your fresh start.*

This is the day that the Lord has made.

Let us rejoice and be glad today!

PSALM 118:24 NCV

*There is wonderful freedom
and joy in coming to recognize
that the fun is in the becoming.*
GLORIA GAITHER

DaySpring

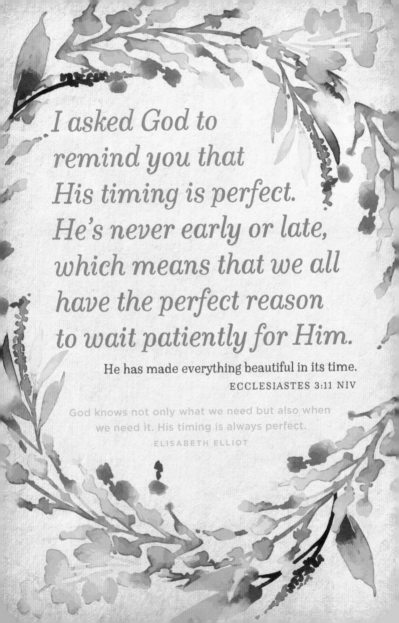

I asked God to
remind you that
His timing is perfect.
He's never early or late,
which means that we all
have the perfect reason
to wait patiently for Him.

He has made everything beautiful in its time.

ECCLESIASTES 3:11 NIV

God knows not only what we need but also when
we need it. His timing is always perfect.

ELISABETH ELLIOT

I asked God to give you this message: You're stronger than you think, and you've got Him on your side. Enough said.

I can do all things through Christ who strengthens me.

PHILIPPIANS 4:13 NKJV

Strive in prayer; let faith fill your heart so will you be strong in the Lord, and in the power of His might.

ANDREW MURRAY

DaySpring

Today, I asked God to give
you strength and courage.
Lots of both.
Know what?
I think He's already
answered my prayer.

*I sought the LORD, and he answered me; he
delivered me from all my fears.*

PSALM 34:4 NIV

Do not limit the limitless God! With Him, face the
future unafraid because you are never alone.

LETTIE COWMAN

DaySpring

I know that the Lord has big plans for you. And He has very important work that only you can do. I'm praying that you and God will make the most of your talents

I urge you to live a life worthy of the calling you have received.

EPHESIANS 4:1 NIV

What we are is God's gift to us.
What we become is our gift to God.

OLD SAYING

DaySpring

Prayer extinguishes worry.
So whenever
you're worried
(or whenever you're not)
it's a good time to pray.

Do not worry about anything, but
pray and ask God for everything you
need, always giving thanks.

PHILIPPIANS 4:6 NCV

Replace worry with prayer.
Make the decision to pray whenever
you catch yourself worrying.
ELIZABETH GEORGE

DaySpring

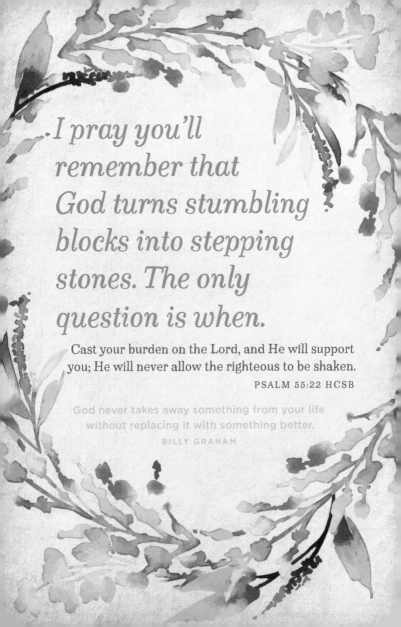

I pray you'll remember that God turns stumbling blocks into stepping stones. The only question is when.

Cast your burden on the Lord, and He will support you; He will never allow the righteous to be shaken.

PSALM 55:22 HCSB

God never takes away something from your life without replacing it with something better.

BILLY GRAHAM

DaySpring

*I asked God to plant
hope and joy in your heart.
God has given us
another day of life.
Let's rejoice and be glad.
Very glad.*

A joyful heart makes a face cheerful.

PROVERBS 15:13 HCSB

Happiness depends on what happens; joy does not.

OSWALD CHAMBERS

DaySpring

I pray you'll remember this:
With God as your partner,
failure is impossible.

———

Those who trust in the Lord are like Mount Zion. It
cannot be shaken; it remains forever.

PSALM 125:1 HCSB

———

God is the silent partner in all great enterprises.
ABRAHAM LINCOLN

I'm praying that you'll turn all your concerns over to God. That way, you can do your best and let Him handle the rest.

Trust in the Lord with all your heart, and lean not on your own understanding; in all your ways acknowledge Him, and He shall direct your paths.

PROVERBS 3:5-6 NKJV

When there is perplexity there is always guidance—not always at the moment we ask, but in good time, which is God's time. There is no need to fret and stew.

ELISABETH ELLIOT

DaySpring

I'm praying that you'll find hope and happiness today. Lots of it. You and I both know it's out there. And I know you can find it.

Those who listen to instruction will prosper;
those who trust the LORD will be happy.

PROVERBS 16:20 NLT

There is never a time when we may not hope in God. Whatever our necessities, however great our difficulties, and though to all appearance help is impossible, yet our business is to hope in God, and it will be found that it is not in vain.

GEORGE MUELLER

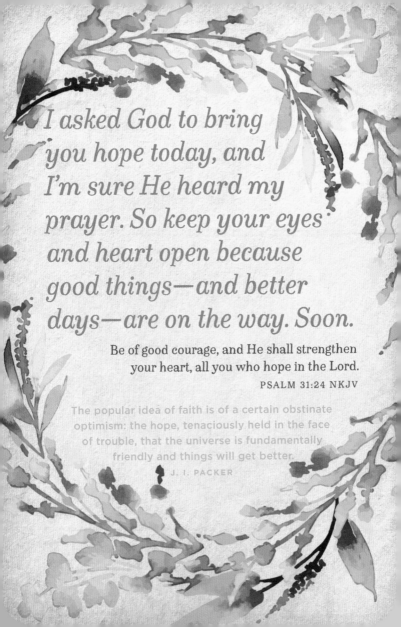

I asked God to bring you hope today, and I'm sure He heard my prayer. So keep your eyes and heart open because good things—and better days—are on the way. Soon.

Be of good courage, and He shall strengthen your heart, all you who hope in the Lord.

PSALM 31:24 NKJV

The popular idea of faith is of a certain obstinate optimism: the hope, tenaciously held in the face of trouble, that the universe is fundamentally friendly and things will get better.

J. I. PACKER

DaySpring

I asked the Lord to remind you that He is your shepherd. He loves you. He's watching over you...and His vision is perfect.

The Lord is my shepherd, I shall not want.
He makes me lie down in green pastures; He leads
me beside quiet waters. He restores my soul.

PSALM 23:1-3 NASB

The Lord God of heaven and earth, the Almighty Creator of all things, He is your Shepherd, and He has charged Himself with the care and keeping of you, as a shepherd is charged with the care and keeping of his sheep.

HANNAH WHITALL SMITH

Whether you realize it or not,
you're surrounded by opportunities.
I asked the Lord to help
you pick the right one.
Or maybe there's more than one.
But don't ask me... ask God.

———

*You will show me the way of life, granting me
the joy of your presence and the pleasures
of living with you forever.*

PSALM 16:11 NLT

———

God uses ordinary people who are obedient
to Him to do extraordinary things.

JOHN MAXWELL

DaySpring

I pray that you'll never forget that each day is a gift. That's why they call it the present.

*So teach us to number our days,
that we may present
to You a heart of wisdom.*

PSALM 90:12 NASB

Every day we live is a priceless gift
of God, loaded with possibilities to learn
something new, to gain fresh insights.

DALE EVANS ROGERS

DaySpring

*I pray that you'll know
how special you are.
The Lord knows that when
He made you, He created
a one-of-a-kind treasure.
I pray you'll know it, too.*

For You formed my inward parts;
You covered me in my mother's womb.
I will praise You, for I am fearfully and
wonderfully made; Marvelous are Your works.

PSALM 139:13-14 NKJV

*Resolve never to criticize or downgrade
yourself, but instead rejoice that you are
fearfully and wonderfully made.*

ELIZABETH GEORGE

DaySpring

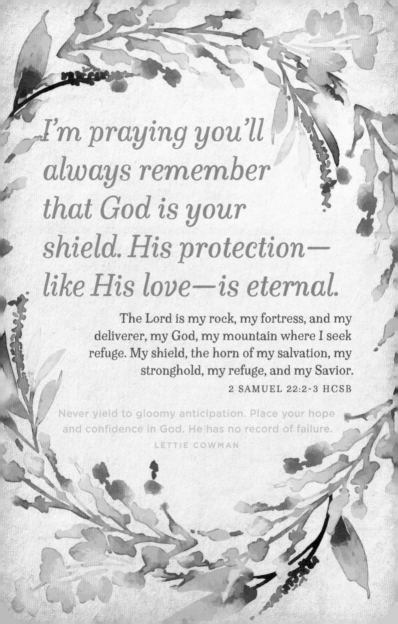

I'm praying you'll always remember that God is your shield. His protection—like His love—is eternal.

The Lord is my rock, my fortress, and my deliverer, my God, my mountain where I seek refuge. My shield, the horn of my salvation, my stronghold, my refuge, and my Savior.

2 SAMUEL 22:2-3 HCSB

Never yield to gloomy anticipation. Place your hope and confidence in God. He has no record of failure.

LETTIE COWMAN

DaySpring

You've got opportunities galore.
I pray that you'll ask God
to help you pick the right one.
With Him, all things
are possible.

But Jesus looked at them and said to them,
"With men this is impossible,
but with God all things are possible."
MATTHEW 19:26 NKJV

Often God shuts a door in our face so that he can open
the door through which he wants us to go.
CATHERINE MARSHALL

DaySpring

I pray that you'll be confident.
With God by your side,
you have every reason to be.

———

But if we look forward to something we don't have
yet, we must wait patiently and confidently.

ROMANS 8:25 NLT

———

Become so wrapped up in something
that you forget to be afraid.

LADY BIRD JOHNSON

DaySpring

I said a prayer for you today,
and I know that God
heard every word.
The Lord wants to lead us
on a path the He chooses.
Our job is to let Him.

Therefore humble yourselves under
the mighty hand of God, that He may
exalt you in due time, casting all your
care upon Him, for He cares for you.

1 PETER 5:6-7 NKJV

It is a joy that God never abandons His children.
He guides faithfully all who listen to His directions.

CORRIE TEN BOOM

DaySpring

True friends are
a gift from above.
You've got friends who love
you and want to help.
I'm one of them....
but not the only one.

Carry one another's burdens;

in this way you will fulfill the law of Christ.

GALATIANS 6:2 HCSB

The measure of a life,
after all, is not its duration
but its donation.
CORRIE TEN BOOM

DaySpring

When you ask
yourself if it's possible,
the answer is, "Maybe."
When you ask God
if it's possible, the answer is,
"Nothing's impossible
for Me." I pray that
you'll trust God.

For with God nothing will be impossible.
LUKE 1:37 NKJV

When God is involved, anything can happen.
CHARLES SWINDOLL

DaySpring

I'm praying for you.
And I'm not the only one.
Plenty of prayers have your
name on the subject line.
Just thought you'd
want to know.

As iron sharpens iron, so people can improve each other.
PROVERBS 27:17 NCV

Friendship, of itself a holy tie, is made more sacred by adversity.
JOHN DRYDEN

DaySpring

Big Picture: IGBOK
(It's Gonna Be OK).
Little Picture: AFSBA
(A Few Speed Bumps Ahead).
My Prayer: TYFOTBP
(That You'll Focus
on the Big Picture).

---

*Let us hold on to the confession of our hope without
wavering, for He who promised is faithful.*

HEBREWS 10:23 HCSB

When you are experiencing the challenges
of life, perspective is everything.

JONI EARECKSON TADA

DaySpring

I pray that you can visualize yourself and God together. Walking together. Working together. Tackling every challenge together. Rejoicing together. Forever.

The Lord says, "I will make you wise and show you where to go. I will guide you and watch over you."

PSALM 32:8 NCV

The beautiful thing about this adventure called faith is that we can count on Him never to lead us astray.

CHARLES SWINDOLL

DaySpring

I said a prayer for you today.
Since I believe in the power
of prayer, I believe in you.
And so, by the way, does God.
Now, I'm praying that
you'll believe in yourself.

That is why we can say with confidence,
"The Lord is my helper, so I will not be
afraid. What can mere mortals do to me?"

HEBREWS 13:6 NLT

*Bible hope is confidence
in the future.*
WARREN WIERSBE

DaySpring

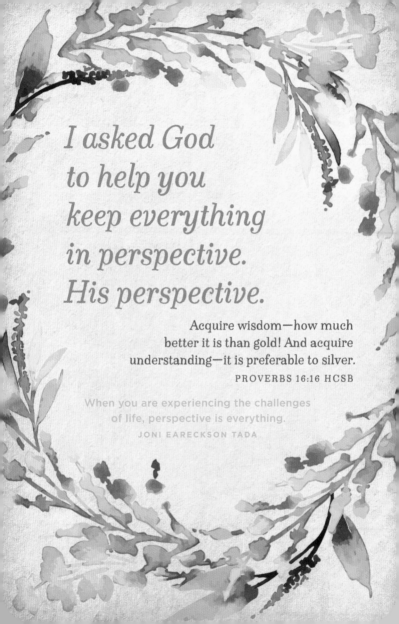

I asked God
to help you
keep everything
in perspective.
His perspective.

Acquire wisdom—how much
better it is than gold! And acquire
understanding—it is preferable to silver.

PROVERBS 16:16 HCSB

When you are experiencing the challenges
of life, perspective is everything.

JONI EARECKSON TADA

DaySpring

I'm praying that
you'll take good care...
very good care...
of a special person...
a very special person
you.

Finally, be strengthened by the Lord and by His vast strength.

EPHESIANS 6:10 HCSB

*Hope can give us life. It can provide energy that would otherwise
do us in completely if we tried to operate in our own strength.*

BARBARA JOHNSON

DaySpring

You and I both know
the power of prayer.
So, I'm praying for
you, and I hope
you'll keep praying
for me.

———

*Rejoice always, pray without ceasing, in
everything give thanks; for this is the
will of God in Christ Jesus for you.*
1 THESSALONIANS 5:16–18 NKJV

———

Any concern that is too small to be turned into a
prayer is too small to be made into a burden.
CORRIE TEN BOOM

DaySpring

I asked God to remind you that tough times never last, but faithful people do... faithful people like you.

Anyone who is having troubles should pray.

JAMES 5:13 NCV

Take courage. We walk in the wilderness today and in the Promised Land tomorrow.

D. L. MOODY

DaySpring

I admire your strength,
but today I asked God
to give you even more.
Do you feel it?
I pray that you do.

He gives strength to the weary,
and to him who lacks might
He increases power.

ISAIAH 40:29 NASB

*Faith is a strong power,
mastering any difficulty
in the strength of the Lord
who made heaven and earth.*
CORRIE TEN BOOM

DaySpring

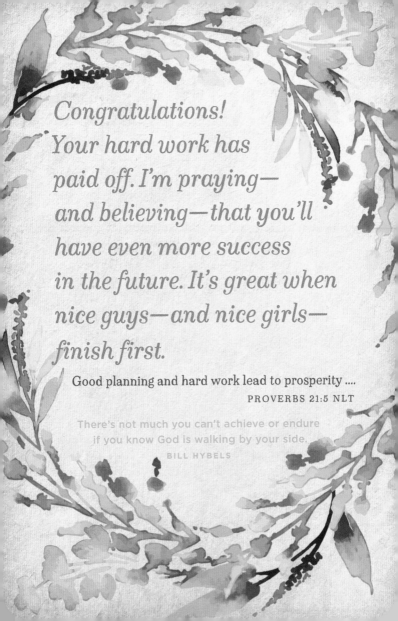

Congratulations! Your hard work has paid off. I'm praying— and believing—that you'll have even more success in the future. It's great when nice guys—and nice girls— finish first.

Good planning and hard work lead to prosperity ....

PROVERBS 21:5 NLT

There's not much you can't achieve or endure
if you know God is walking by your side.

BILL HYBELS

DaySpring

I asked God to give you more courage today. Maybe you already have enough, but I figured a little more can't hurt.

The Lord is my light and my salvation; whom shall I fear?
The Lord is the strength of my life; of whom shall I be afraid?

PSALM 27:1 NKJV

*When God speaks, oftentimes His voice will call
for an act of courage on our part.*

CHARLES STANLEY

DaySpring

I asked God to
remind you that
no challenges are
too big for Him.
Even big problems are
no problem for God.

———

For whatsoever is born of God
overcometh the world…
1 JOHN 5:4 KJV

———

God will make obstacles serve His purpose.
LETTIE COWMAN

You've worked so hard, and it shows. I'm praying—and believing—that your hard work will be rewarded. Soon!

Be strong and courageous, and do the work. Don't be afraid or discouraged by the size of the task, for the LORD God, my God, is with you. He will not fail you or forsake you.

1 CHRONICLES 28:20 NLT

It may be that the day of judgment will dawn tomorrow; in that case, we shall gladly stop working for a better future. But not before.

DIETRICH BONHOEFFER

Love never ends.
So I'm praying
that you'll remember
we love you.
Always.

No one has ever seen God.
If we love one another, God remains
in us and His love is perfected in us.

1 JOHN 4:12 HCSB

The best use of life is love.
The best expression of love is time. The
best time to love is now.

RICK WARREN

DaySpring

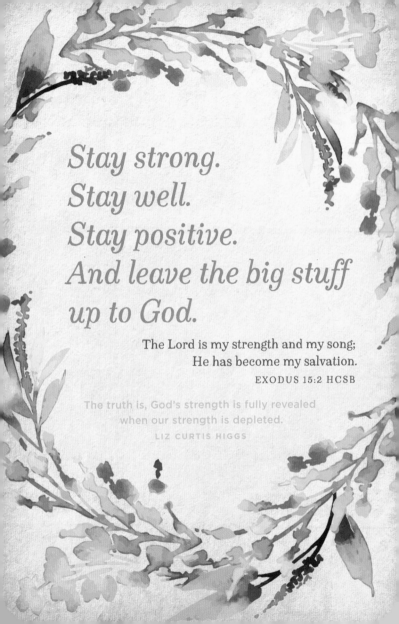

Stay strong.
Stay well.
Stay positive.
And leave the big stuff
up to God.

The Lord is my strength and my song;
He has become my salvation.

EXODUS 15:2 HCSB

The truth is, God's strength is fully revealed
when our strength is depleted.

LIZ CURTIS HIGGS

DaySpring

Today, I told God
that I'm thankful for you.
He knew it already.
And now, you know it, too.

Give thanks to the Lord, for He is good;
His faithful love endures forever.
PSALM 118:29 HCSB

*Fill up the spare moments of your life
with praise and thanksgiving.*
SARAH YOUNG

DaySpring

I said a prayer for you today.
I asked God
to remind you that faith
is stronger than fear.
Focus on your faith, and
your fears will fade away.
Fast.

Be not afraid; only believe.

MARK 5:36 NKJV

Faith expects from God what is
beyond all expectation.

ANDREW MURRAY

DaySpring

I pray that you'll always ask God for the things you need. He's always listening, and He always wants to hear from you. Now.

Keep asking, and it will be given to you. Keep searching, and you will find. Keep knocking, and the door will be opened to you. For everyone who asks receives, and the one who searches finds, and to the one who knocks, the door will be opened.

MATTHEW 7:7-8 HCSB

Don't be afraid to ask your heavenly Father for anything you need. Indeed, nothing is too small for God's attention or too great for his power.

DENNIS SWANBERG

DaySpring

I'm praying for you
and your family.
I'm sure you're praying, too,
but when it comes to prayer,
more is better.

Rejoice in hope; be patient
in affliction; be persistent in prayer.

ROMANS 12:12 HCSB

We must leave it to God to answer
our prayers in His own wisest way.
Sometimes, we are so impatient
and think that God does not answer.
God always answers!
He never fails! Be still.
Abide in Him.

LETTIE COWMAN

DaySpring

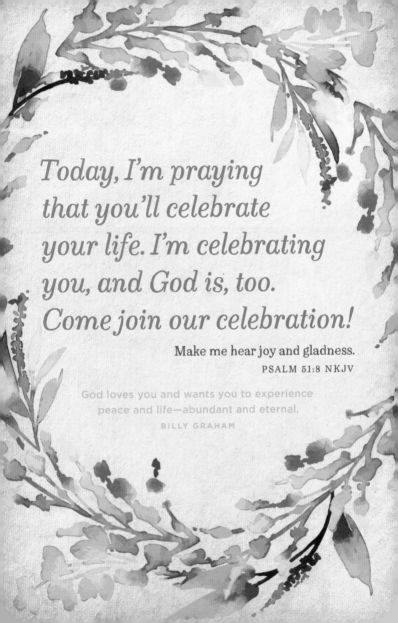

Today, I'm praying that you'll celebrate your life. I'm celebrating you, and God is, too. Come join our celebration!

Make me hear joy and gladness.
PSALM 51:8 NKJV

God loves you and wants you to experience peace and life—abundant and eternal.
BILLY GRAHAM

*I asked God to give you
strength for your journey,
and I'm sure He heard my prayer.
Better days are coming.
Soon.*

Be strong and courageous,
for your work will be rewarded.
2 CHRONICLES 15:7 NLT

*Strive in prayer; let faith fill your heart so will you be
strong in the Lord, and in the power of His might.*

ANDREW MURRAY

DaySpring

Optimism pays.
Pessimism costs.
I pray—and believe—
that your amazing optimism
will pay big dividends.
Keep it up!

This hope we have as an anchor of the soul,
a hope both sure and steadfast.

HEBREWS 6:19 NASB

Developing a positive attitude means
working continually to find what is
uplifting and encouraging.

BARBARA JOHNSON

DaySpring

Today, I asked God to give
you hope and confidence.
It's a new day, and
I'm praying for you.
I'll help any way I can.
And, God will, too.

*Do not remember the former things,
nor consider the things of old.
Behold, I will do a new thing.*

ISAIAH 43:18-19 NKJV

God specializes in giving people a fresh start.

RICK WARREN

I pray that you'll remember this: God's got everything under control, so there's no need to panic. Ever.

As for God, His way is perfect;
the word of the Lord is proven;
He is a shield to all who trust in Him.

PSALM 18:30 NKJV

God has no problems, only plans. There is never panic in heaven.
CORRIE TEN BOOM

DaySpring

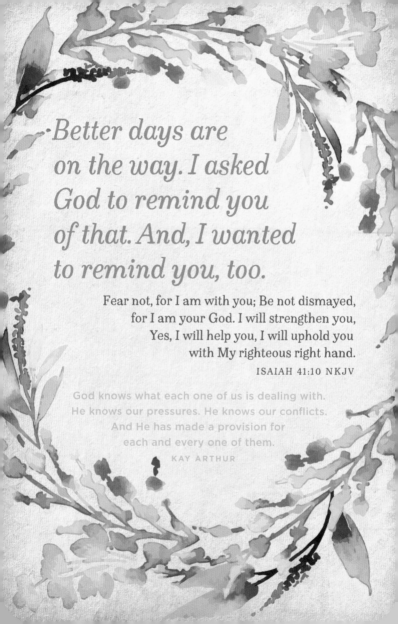

Better days are on the way. I asked God to remind you of that. And, I wanted to remind you, too.

Fear not, for I am with you; Be not dismayed, for I am your God. I will strengthen you, Yes, I will help you, I will uphold you with My righteous right hand.

ISAIAH 41:10 NKJV

God knows what each one of us is dealing with. He knows our pressures. He knows our conflicts. And He has made a provision for each and every one of them.

KAY ARTHUR

DaySpring

I pray that you'll take it day by day, one day at a time, in day-tight compartments. Tough times never last, but patient people do.

The Lord is wonderfully good to those who wait for him and seek him. So it is good to wait quietly for salvation from the Lord.

LAMENTATIONS 3:25-26 NLT

Every heavy burden you are called upon to lift hides within itself a miraculous secret of strength.

LETTIE COWMAN

DaySpring

I'm praying for you, and it's working. You're getting stronger every day. The Lord knows it, and I know it, and you probably know it, too. But it never hurts to be reminded.

Have faith in the Lord your God, and you will stand strong. Have faith in his prophets, and you will succeed.

2 CHRONICLES 20:20 NCV

The strength that we claim from God's Word does not depend on circumstances. Circumstances will be difficult, but our strength will be sufficient.

CORRIE TEN BOOM

I'm praying
that you'll be hopeful...
and that you'll stay positive...
and that you'll never forget
I love you.

When doubts filled my mind,
your comfort gave me
renewed hope and cheer.

PSALM 94:19 NLT

Be hopeful! For tomorrow
has never happened before.

ROBERT SCHULLER

I asked God
to remind you that nothing
is impossible for Him.
When we've done all we can,
He takes over.

For with God nothing
will be impossible.

LUKE 1:37 NKJV

God is able to do what we can't.

BILLY GRAHAM

DaySpring

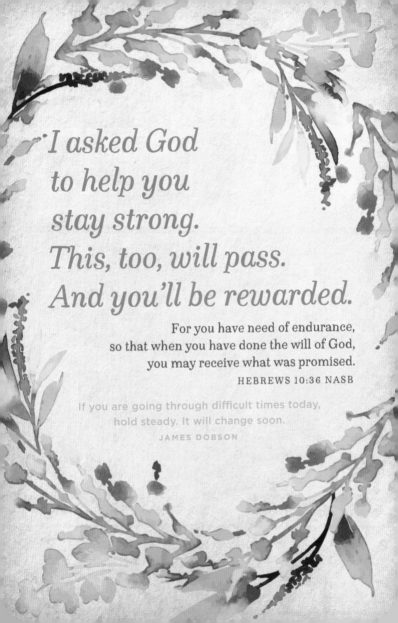

I asked God
to help you
stay strong.
This, too, will pass.
And you'll be rewarded.

For you have need of endurance,
so that when you have done the will of God,
you may receive what was promised.

HEBREWS 10:36 NASB

If you are going through difficult times today,
hold steady. It will change soon.

JAMES DOBSON

Stay positive. Very Positive. I'm praying—and I truly believe—that the better days will be here sooner than you think.

The Lord is my light and my salvation—
so why should I be afraid? The Lord protects me
from danger—so why should I tremble?

PSALM 27:1 NLT

*The sermon of your life in tough times ministers to people
more powerfully than the most eloquent speaker.*

BILL BRIGHT

I asked God to remind you
that patience pays.
And that it's going to pay
for you.

———

*But if we hope for what we do not yet
have, we wait for it patiently.*

ROMANS 8:25 NIV

———

Teach us, O Lord, the disciplines of patience, for
to wait is often harder than to work.

PETER MARSHALL

If God had a refrigerator, your picture would be on it. His love for you is infinite and eternal. That's a massive amount of love that lasts forever. So don't worry—be hopeful, happy, and grateful.

For the Lord is good. His unfailing love continues forever, and his faithfulness continues to each generation.

PSALM 100:5 NLT

God. There is no limit to His power. There is no limit to His love. There is no limit to His mercy.

BILLY GRAHAM

*Today,
as I said my prayers,
I told God I was
grateful for you.
And I wanted
to tell you.*

A friend loves you all the time,
and a brother helps in time of trouble.

PROVERBS 17:17 NCV

*It is only with gratitude
that life becomes rich.*
DIETRICH BONHOEFFER

I pray that you'll always remember this formula: God's strength + your trust = victory.

I lift up my eyes to the hills—where does my help come from? My help comes from the LORD, the Maker of heaven and earth.

PSALM 121:1-2 NIV

Trust God's Word and His power more than you trust your own feelings and experiences. Remember, your Rock is Christ, and it is the sea that ebbs and flows with the tides, not Him.

LETTIE COWMAN

DaySpring

God already knows that I'm praying for your speedy recovery. Now you know it, too.

I lift up my eyes to the hills—where does
my help come from? My help comes
from the LORD, the Maker of heaven and earth.

PSALM 121:1-2 NIV

God's power is great enough for our deepest desperation.
You can go on. You can pick up the pieces and start anew. You
can face your fears. There is healing for your soul.

SUZANNE DALE EZELL

DaySpring

You've come a long way.
Today, I asked God
to remind you how much
you've already accomplished.
And the best is yet to come.

"I say this because I know what I am
planning for you," says the Lord. "I have
good plans for you, not plans to hurt you.
I will give you hope and a good future."
JEREMIAH 29:11 NCV

Remember how far you've come, not just how far
you have to go. You are not where you want
to be, but neither are you where you used to be.
RICK WARREN

DaySpring